A Reading by Judy Grahn Upon the Founding of

Homodoxy

April 2026

www.commonalityinstitute.org

www.homodoxy.com

ISBN: 978-1-7370833-1-3

Introduction

my mother is a pastor and my father is a publisher and my sister is a dancer and my friends are poets and theologians and my family comes from other countries and speaks other tongues and my first lover chose to be celibate but is no longer celibate and my second lover is still a friend and we have a spark that never catches but still sustains an energy across distance and my third lover was a sower but I was also a sower and this has nothing to do with sexual positions but our garden never blossomed and my fourth and briefer lover gave everything in weekends that couldn't sustain me and with each of these men I shared no more than three months of bright intensity and throughout and between them all were many more and briefer lovers who have been artists and scholars and engineers and not enough architects and one lived on a tiny island with his partner for a year or two and one photographed Celine Dion and nursed me through a night of terror and one taught me how to fist him and one touched me during the pandemic when no one touched no one and one was an opera singer who ghosted me repeatedly and I allowed it because he made me shiver and several of them have been younger men who want to be my boy or wife and want me to be daddy and I want to be daddy but the domestic fantasy has only ever yielded more fantasy but maybe this time or maybe now and my desire is not as capacious as I want it to be but it is capacious enough and my dyke friends are stabler and my priest friends are my sisters and in my long long education I did not treat my teachers formally enough because I could see how they too could be my siblings and I would rather be that than a future colleague and I am not following them into traditional professorial work because I have seen the strains it puts on people and because I have seen the fickleness of the institutions that have educated us and I have seen how the theologies of those institutions would demand that my work be something other than this long and intricate thread that connects the fullness of my words to that of my faith and tits and lovers and thanks to my teachers I have found an uncompromising will within me that shocks me daily and while it is often said that one should not meet one's heroes I have insisted on meeting the writers and publishers who have become my heroes because AIDS killed a lot of them but some are still alive so I have insisted on meeting my heroes and without realizing this is what I've been doing I've insisted that they bless me and some of them have blessed me with advice and encouragement and blurbs and even the odd curse which is still a blessing because words don't lose their miracle easily and all of this became my heart and I can't be faithful to my heart without trying to bless like I have been blessed and this means setting holy fire to the stories we are given but in my cave of wonders which is the name my dad gave to the basement where he wrote his dissertation on St. Athanasius's use of scripture while my mom wrote sermons a floor above him and my sister choreographed and I a child dreamed dreams and screamed screams I never dreamt I'd make a cave of wonders of my own but it became the name I use to describe the head space in which I write when the words build up enough to pour out and the living room in New Haven in which type sometimes roasting sometimes freezing and yes in my cave of wonders writing about theology and AIDS I have become so accustomed to living with the dead that when I am able to speak with the living what a joy what a joy joy joy and on a whim one day I wrote to Judy Grahn through the contact form on her website and I did not know if she would answer I just knew that when I read *Another Mother Tongue* and she called herself a "ceremonial dyke" I knew that I was one too or a ceremonial faggot and I knew she had cofounded a press to publish women's words about women because she loved women and I knew some of her books are now hard to find and I was already thinking that I should start a press for gay theology and literature and maybe maybe she would let me do a new edition of *Another Mother Tongue* and when Judy responded to my inquiry I nearly jumped through my skin clearly it can be a dark world that we live in but she is kind she is she is she is she is is is a soft butch and a seer she is a beloved word smith and a lover she is an Amazon and a river she forges whole worlds with her fingers and in her worlds words work wonders and through her words ancient wisdom thunders and by this wisdom new life wanders into forms yet to be discovered and in my hand now are her words and in your hand now are our words and in whose hands will you place your words your lover teacher sister mother father brother publisher pastor or another

Samuel Ernest

I’m not a girl

I’m not a girl
I’m a hatchet
I’m not a hole
I’m a whole mountain
I’m not a fool
I’m a survivor
I’m not a pearl
I’m the Atlantic Ocean
I’m not a good lay
I’m a straight razor
Look at me as if you had never seen a woman before
I have red, red hands and much bitterness

She Who continues

She Who continues
She Who has a being
named She Who is a being
named She Who carries her own name.
She Who turns things over.
She Who marks her own way, gathering.
She Who makes her own difference.
She Who differs, gathering her own events.
She Who gathers, gaining
She Who carries her own ways,
gathering She Who waits,
bearing She Who cares for her
own name, carrying She Who
bears, gathering She Who cares
for She Who gathers her own ways,
carrying
the names of She Who gather and gain,
singing: I am the woman, the woman
              the woman - I am the first person.
and the first person is She Who is the first person to
She Who is the first person to no other. There is no
other first person.

She Who floods like a river and
like a river continues
She Who continues

you are what is female

you are what is female
you shall be called Eve.
and what is masculine shall be called God.

And from you name Eve we shall take
the word Evil.
and from God's, the word Good.
now you understand patriarchal morality.

The Marilyn Monroe Poem

I have come to claim
Marilyn Monroe's body
for the sake of my own.
dig it up, hand it over,
cram it in this paper sack.
hubba. hubba. hubba.
look at those luscious
long brown bones, that wide and crusty
pelvis. ha HA, oh she wanted so much to be serious

but she never stops smiling now.
Has she lost her mind?

Marilyn, be serious—they're taking
your picture, and they're taking the pictures
of eight young women in New York City
who murdered themselves for being pretty
by the same method as you, the very
next day, after you!
I have claimed their bodies too,
they smile up out of my paper sack
like brainless cinderellas.

the reporters are furious, they're asking
me questions
what right does a woman have
to Marilyn Monroe's body? and what
am I doing for lunch? They think I
mean to eat you. Their teeth are lurid

and they want to pose me, leaning
on the shovel, nude. Don't squint.

But when one of the reporters comes too close
I beat him, bust his camera
with your long, smooth thigh
and with your lovely knucklebone
I break his eye.

Long ago you wanted to write poems;
Be serious, Marilyn
I am going to take you in this paper sack
around the world, and
write on it:—the poems of Marilyn Monroe—
Dedicated to all princes,
the male poets who were so sorry to see you go,
before they had a crack at you.
They wept for you, and also
they wanted to stuff you
while you still had a little meat left
in useful places;
but they were too slow.

Now I shall take them my paper sack
and we shall act out a poem together:
"How would you like to see Marilyn Monroe,
in action, smiling, and without her clothes?"
We shall wait long enough to see them make familiar faces
and then I shall beat them with your skull.

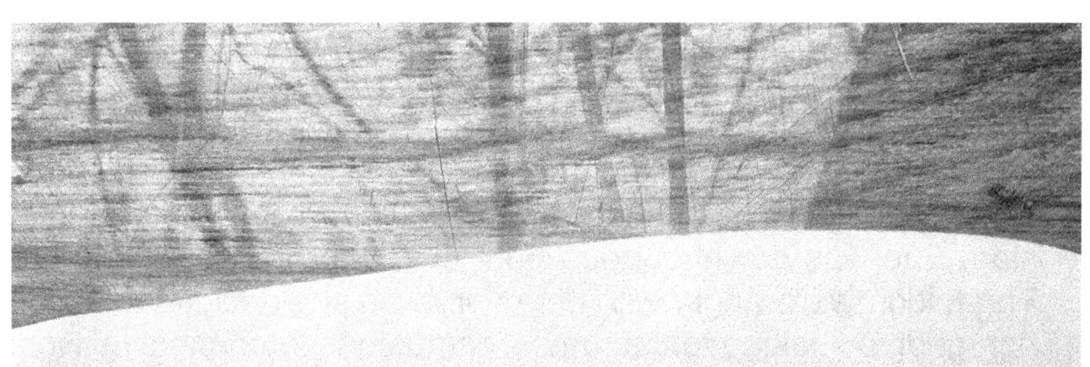

hubba. hubba. hubba. hubba. hubba.
Marilyn, be serious
Today I have come to claim your body for my own.

1000 B.C., The Amazons at the Battle of Troy

Penthesilea, Amazon queen, had accidentally killed her own sister Hippolyta in a hunting expedition with a spear intended for a stag. She was downhearted about this, and her sister warriors of Thremidon were angry with her over it. So she decided to assuage her grief by taking on a battle campaign. According to Donald Sobol's version of the story, she arrived one day with twelve stalwart maiden warriors to the great siege of Troy, then in its tenth year, and offered the city her help. The Trojans were ecstatic that the fabulous warrior Penthesilea had come, all the more so because they had just lost their brightest star, King Priam's son Hector, in a hand-to-hand contest with the Greek Achilles, whose mother had dipped him in the River Styx to render him invincible.

Long angry with the Greeks for defeats her own army had suffered because of wars waged on them by the Greek heroes Belerophon, Heracles, and Theseus, Penthesilea stood in the hall of the Trojans with no doubts about her own motives. She addressed the royal company, who included the king and queen, Priam and Hecuba, and also the gorgeous Helen, Queen of Sparta, whose illicit love of Prince Paris was said to be the cause of the arduous and bloody war, of the 1,186 ships and 100,000 men led by her angry husband, Menelaus, surrounding the city.

Penthesilea, hand on hip and head thrown back, promised to turn the war around in favor of the Trojans with her twelve warriors and her own fierce right arm. She promised to rout the Greeks one by one and to leave even their invincible Achilles, terror of the plains, groveling in his own innards. She promised to send the men running to their ships, grateful to get away from Troy with their skins intact.

The Trojans of the royal house stood and cheered, for they lived on hope, and she and all her kind had such a fearsome reputation. The Greeks for a thousand years after would say that of all the old-world armies they went up against, all of the monsters, supernatural sorcerers, giants, horsemen – the Amazons of Thermidon, the women warriors, were the bravest and most difficult, the most memorable, the most beautiful, the most worthy to be called a foe.

Queen Helen and Queen Penthesilea toasted each other and exchanged looks that night, the one so curiously passive as her husband railed at the gate to regain her person by force, the other who had come, trained all her life to take up arms with him on his wife's behalf.

In the morning Penthesilea dressed meticulously in a rainbow-colored corselet. She wrapped her athlete's legs in light gold armor leggings and put on a gold helmet with long streamers. Her flashing sword, cased in a scabbard of ivory and silver, hung over one shoulder. Over her left arm she slid the crescent shield of the moon-maidens of Thermidon. In her left hand she gripped two javelins and in her right hand the double-edged ax of the old gynarchy she represented. Then with her similarly dressed twelve warriors around her she rallied the Trojan men and led them all onto the field that lay before the city. Thus she went up against the young, all-male Greek army.

The names of her warriors were Clonie, Polemusa, Thermodosa, Harmothoe, Derione, Evandre, Antandre, Bremusa, Hippothoe, Harmothoe, Alcibie, Derimacheia, and Antibrote, each seasoned in battle and fierce in reputation. It was their last campaign, the last of the Amazons who had their own territory.

They went out against the Greek army who outnumbered them and all the citizens of Troy by ten to one, and yet the women were so fierce they left all the soil around Troy red with the blood they hewed out of the soldiers. As the afternoon bore on and other Amazons fell around her, nothing could withstand Penthesilea as she taunted and struck, struck and taunted. Achilles, had his mother not given him his magical protection, could never have withstood her. But he did have magical protection, and he not only withstood her, letting her tremendous spear throws crash off his armor, he slew her. And in the sculpted art through all the centuries of conquest, just as there would be "The Last Indian" and

"The Dying Gaul," so there would be "The Wounded Amazon," the beautiful fallen warrior, Penthesilea.

And as she lay dying, Achilles decided that he "loved" her. Seeing the warrior stilled, seeing the blood run from wounds in her body, he became excited. Seeing her female might conquered by his own hand, he raped her. And when a fellow soldier protested this peculiar behavior toward a military enemy, Achilles chopped the soldier's head off. The sorrowing Trojans pulled Penthesilea's body from the river where the Greeks had thrown it. They gave Queen Penthesilea a hera's funeral and buried her in a special mound, her fallen warriors buried close around her. Troy went down soon after and was burnt, its women captured. Menelaus took his wife, Queen Helen, to her homeland as a slave; and she was soon murdered by her nephew. The gynarchic rule had crumbled, and a new wave of authority had arisen to establish patriarchal rule. In our age this rule has ripened and is beginning the decline that will give rise to a new cycle.

What matters about the Amazons is not that they fought and not that they lost – as thousands of armies have done before and since – but *what* they lost and how they lost. That they lost the Thermidon and their cities and their Libyan queendoms. That they lost their belt, the belt of female power, the blood-power girdle. And that they lost each other. And that Penthesilea was raped, her very soul stolen as she lay dying. And this was for her "beauty," he said, that is, he wanted her very life force, her sexual essence. So they lost, the women-warriors, the warriors for women: their territory, their single-minded sisterhood, their magical power, their autonomy of their bodies.

Nor have we regained these since the Trojan War, losing them over and over, nor have we stopped trying to regain them, nor have we stopped understanding that it will be done.

I first met the Queen of Wands

I first met the Queen of Wands in a 1913 translation of a clay tablet of ancient Babylonian writing, that wedge-shaped cuneiform record from the ancient Middle East that is like the footprints of birds.

The text of the tablet, called "A Tablet of Lamentation," begins chillingly: "the cow wailed, and in her place she lay down." The story is of a queen who has been stolen from her temple and carried away by ship. "My temple thou art not," she wails in grief. She has been stolen from her city, her people and her land, by an unknown and unnamed enemy called by her, "The Foe." Coming by ship, he strips off her clothing and jewelry, and carries her away into slavery on his vessel. This theme of a queen who has been stolen, of cities and temples ravaged by soldiers, of people cudgeled in their streets, of lamentation for a female power gone, is a repeated one, especially among mid-Eastern cuneiform tablets of the period around 2500 B.C.

Moved by the tale told in the Tablet of Lamentation, I searched for other stories of stolen queens, wanting to identify this one with a name, occupation, some motive for the theft. The most persistently retold story of a queen stolen in Western tradition is that recounted in *The Iliad*. In this story the queen is Helen, Queen of Sparta and known as Helen of Troy, where a furious war was fought over her person. Her face was later described as so beautiful as to be, "The face that launched a thousand ships." She was hated and blamed for the most famous war of western history and literature, the model war of Troy.

In investigating Helen's story I found an astonishingly worldwide myth of a female god of beauty, fire, love, light, thought and weaving. She is a figure of many forms and names and countries, and she is the Queen of Wands.

After identifying her as a weaver I was carried back, so far back in time that an ancient spirit presented itself to me for the purposes of my story. This spirit is a weaving spider, a fate spinner from whose very body comes the cloth of life and time and understanding. I named this spirit *webster,* or Spider Webster. Webster is a word that formerly meant "female weaver," the "ster" ending indicating a female ancestor, or female possession of the word.

The word-weavers of recent centuries who have given us the oration of Daniel Webster and the dictionary listings of Merriam-Webster stem from English family names that once descended through the female line. Some great-great grandmother gave them her last name, *Webster,* she-who-weaves. In this story of the Queen of Wands, webster is a spider/spirit, often quite immense (in the woods, the moonlight; peering over the horizon with a sun-like eye) albeit she is also often tiny, lurking in the corners and shadows of our all-glistening, aluminum world. If the webster of dictionary fame comes first to your mind when you see Spider Webster's name, remember that she gave the surname to him, as well as giving the words. For language is a form of weaving too, a clothing our ideas wear, a glowing flesh they are made of, a heart that beats in them.

They say she is veiled

They say she is veiled
and a mystery.   That is
one way of looking.
Another
is that she is where
she always has been, exactly in place,
and it is we,
we who are mystified,
we who are veiled
and without faces.

Helen in Hollywood

When she goes to Hollywood
she is an angel.

She writes in red red lipstick
on the window of her body,
long for me, oh need me!
Parts her lips like a lotus.

Opening night she stands, poised
on her carpet, luminescent,
young men humming
all around her. She is flying.
Her high heels are wands, her
furs electric. Her bracelets
flashing. How completely
dazzling her complexion,
how vibrant her hair and eyes,
how brilliant the glow that spreads
four full feet around her.

She is totally self conscious
self contained
self centered,
caught in the blazing central eye
of our attention.

We infuse her.
Fans, we wave at her
like handmaids, unabashedly,
we crowd on tiptoe pressed together
just to feel the fission of the star
that lives on earth,

the bright, the angel sun
the luminescent glow of someone
other than we.
Look! Look! She is different.
Medium for all our energy
as we pour it through her.
Vessel of light.
Her flesh is like flax,
a living fiber.
She is the symbol of our dreams and fears
and bloody visions, all
our metaphors for living in America.

Harlowe, Holiday, Monroe

Helen
when she goes to Hollywood
she is the fire for all purposes.

Her flesh is like dark wax, a candle.
She is from any place or class.
"That's the one," we say in instant recognition,
because our breath is taken by her beauty,
or what we call her beauty.

She is glowing from every pore.
we adore her. we imitate and rob her
adulate envy
admire neglect
scorn. leave alone
invade, fill
ourselves with her.
we love her, we say
and if she isn't careful
we may even kill her.

Opening night
she lands on her carpet,
long fingered hands
like divining rods
bobbing and drawing the strands
of our attention,
as limousine drivers in blue jackets
stand on the hoods of their cars
to see the angel, talking

Davis, Dietrich, Wood
Tyson, Taylor, Gabor
Helen, when she goes to Hollywood
to be a walking star,
to be an actor

She is far more than a product
of Max Factor,
Max Factor didn't make her
though the make-up helps us
see what we would like
to take her for

her flesh is like glass,
a chandelier
a mirror

Harlowe, Holiday, Monroe
Helen
when she went to Hollywood
to be an angel

And it is she and not we
who is different

She who marries the crown prince
who leads the processional dance,
she who sweeps eternally
down the steps
in her long round gown.
A leaping, laughing leading lady,
she is our flower.
It is she who lies strangled
in the bell tower;
she who is monumentally drunk and suicidal
or locked waiting in the hightower,
she who lies sweating with the vicious jungle fever,
who leaps from her blue window
when he will, if he will, leave her

it is she and not we
who is the lotus

It is she with the lilies in her hair
and a keyboard beside her,
the dark flesh glowing

She whose wet lips nearly swallow
the microphone, whose whiskey voice
is precise and sultry and overwhelming,
she who is princess and harlequin,
athlete and moll and whore and lady,
goddess of the silver screen
the only original American queen

and Helen
when she was an angel
when she went to Hollywood

Helen's names

Helen has such a lengthy history
as a god and as a queen
that her name, El-Ana, has derivations
and echoes that are widespread over
continents. The Muhammedan Venus is called
Anael, which has the syllables of
El-Ana reversed. From El comes Bella
meaning "beauty."
Beulah Ann is one variation,
as are Helena, Helga, Holga, Helda,
Hilda, Holde, Hillary, Helna, Hildegard,
Helle. Hlin. Hlinda, Linda. Honnele.
Heleme.
Yelana, El-Inna, Lil-Ana, Lilly Anne,
Lou Anne, Lillian. Angelina.
El-Luna, Elna, Elanya
Elana. Hannah Belle
Annabel, Belle Anna, Belana,
Helana, Elaina, Elaine
Eleanor, Eileen, Alienor
Hela, Nina, Lenora, Lee Anna, Leona
Nona, Ilona, Lena
Ellen, Ella, Ellie
Nellie, Nell. Hel-Aine,
Helaine.
Lena, Lana, Lanya
Helanya.
Hello, Helanya.

Beauty, sleeping (Who shall wake us)

Who shall wake us
if we don't ourselves
shake loose the sleep
of ages, animate the doll
at last and bid her
rise, and move and rule.

Who will wake us from our
dream of capture
if we don't ourselves
shake loose the long spell,
the illusion of being small
and silenced, sourceless
and unheated.

Who will be all knowing
and the prince if *we* don't
make him happen, somehow
groom him for his task
to rouse us from the suicidal
slumber.

(And the Foe if no one else
knows how to shine his boots
knows how to stride
to the tower steps
and rocket up to shake us
from our sleepy lives
with fear. But I don't mean
the Foe, I mean another
and ourselves)

Let the prince come
integrated and sure
let it be time
for a man strong in his
insides
without boots or
a broken brain, let him
have a golden net
around him

Let him arrive now
in any form, as a Bear God
or computer programmer
or even a dyke in a man's costume
let his step resonate the steps
of the hightower

Mothers mothers raise him
tell him, make him
who will wake us
who will wake us
who will wake us from our
trance of ages
if we don't

Ourselves prepare
for that reception;
animate the doll's flesh
for the kiss of life
of recognition,
animate the doll's will at last
and bid her rise
and move, and rule

My attention was drawn to the person of Helen when Bella Vivante (Zweig) offered a course on her as both goddess and queen. Reading Homer, Euripides, Sappho and H.D., I engaged with the archetypal character of Helen as "work" and also as "wisdom" since she is related to the Gnostic Feminine principle of Sophia.

I see all my mythic-based work as a continuation of my love for working class voices, (so I call it mythic realism) and with *The Queen of Wands* I am conscientiously criss-crossing time and space barriers to create a Helen who lives both in her history and also in the now, and is immanent in real people. So I have attempted to shatter the myth into a kaleidoscope of possible "Helens." Helen has been most often associated with upperclass and "white" standards of beauty, and with queenship, with being a goddess, with causing a great war; but her history is much more interesting than that; she is a woman who takes a fall, rises, takes a fall again; and who is sometimes at the height of power and glory and sometimes at the lowest end of the social scale—she is both goddess and slut, queen and slave, and in my version, she is also ordinary working women/people. Her "beauty" is so many values we can love or desire, including freedom; it is also the life energy that every worker contributes to the acts of living in a "factory" world.

This reminds us that any person or nation can be captured (or transfixed) in a tyranny whose grasp can be broken only through conscious concerted action.

"Who shall wake us if we don't ourselves?" "Mothers mothers raise him/ tell him, make him/ . . . who will wake us/ from our trance of ages/ if we don't ourselves . . ."

Dancing in Place

Oh Lady, Lady of the changing shapes
help me remember
how to dance in place;
when to witness,
when to harness,
when to charge with all my forces.

I don’t know the reaches of my fate.
I know your shadow falls across my face.

Oh Lady, Lady of the Great Bolow.
Hard are your lessons,
many-fanged your harshness;
irresistible are your passions
and sweet, sweet are your praises.

I don’t know the mazes of your soul.
I know your shadow falls beside me
everywhere I go.

philosophers, songwriters and filmmakers of our generation take note and write more appropriate versions of the myths.

Mythic realism seeks to challenge universal or static and disempowering myths of Western culture by using and transforming them into vital energized stories as possibilities for both women in particular and people in general. The tactic is one of shattering the original myth to produce new variants. I then attempt to hold these variations within a ritual drama that reveals facets. Realism, in the sense of contemporary and historic stories, (including pieces of my personal story) can thus engage the primal myth-stuff, merge with it and give it renewed life, emotion and meaning. The myth of Helen of Troy is particularly compelling because she already has so many facets, and was born of an egg, in a version in which her mother is Leda, a swan. The Troy story refers to a major war of Greeks against Trojans; they were fighting over the autonomy of Helen, who had left her Greek husband for a Trojan lover named Paris. I began my extensive journey with her in *The Queen of Wands* (1982) and continued in *The Queen of Swords*, 1987) casting her further back in time as Inanna, the Mesopotamian Venus of four to five thousand years ago. This second book- length poem utilizes the plot of recently translated Mesopotamian poetry, infusing ancient yet eerily familiar myths into my version. I modernized Helen in *Swords* by setting the scene in an underworld lesbian bar of contemporary times and letting a bunch of rather raucous characters, including the Amazon Warrior Penthesilea, who fought for her at Troy, put the modern Helen through a major transformation.

In a sense I have taken the literary idea "Helen" (as the beauty of all women) and splattered her as if she were an egg, except each splatter has a regenerative quality; they are not identical but they have the same substance. Beads of mercury do this when dropped; the central ball breaks into dozens of other balls, each having the same qualities of the original, and made of the same substance; and if you split each one again, they would again form smaller droplets with the same qualities as the original. *That* is the Helen I am imagining, not a single archetype—but instead a multicharacter, infinitely immanent, who crosses time and space, who lives simultaneously in "all of us."

Helen as a Goddess, El-Ana, Keeper of the Flame, House of Fire

Until recent times, an annual festival honoring Helen as an ancient creation God was held on the Greek island of Rhodes. She was worshipped and represented in the form of a tree. In Hebrew tradition she was Ashera; for the Ainu people of Japan she is Ashketanne-mat; for Sumerians she was Anait.

The birthday of the sun is winter solstice, December 21. In northern climates she is celebrated as the tree with lights. The blessed Mary's mother was Anne or Anna, Grandmother of Christ on his mother's side, the distaff side of the family. Ana means life, source, womb. Sometimes the word is *ama* instead of ana. The Sun Goddess of Japan is Ama-terasu. Hannah-hannah means the Grandmother in Chaldean. Hame Haa is a Pueblo Indian word, "in the place of the Grandmother," meaning time eons past, "long ago so far."

In various languages ana means life, altar, sustenance, grace. Ana means womb, and most of the words applying to woman and to the female Gods mean womb. *Gyne,* the Greek for woman, is the base of the word queen. Venus, beauty, means vulva. Ana-Yana-Yoni-Ioni-Gyne-Cune-Cwen-Queen.

In Tuareg tribes of North Africa, still matrilineal in descent, the title for mother is Anna, and for daughter, Yell. Anna-yell, Ana-el, El-Ana, Helena, "beauty." The Sun Goddess underlying Greek culture was Helen or Helena and she was much much older than Greek civilization.

El-Ana, Flame-womb, House of Fire, Thought Woman. El, creative fire, is present in words such as electric and element, and also in Ilium (the city of Troy), city of the Sun, Ile. On this continent, the Lakota Indian word Ile (Elay) means Flame. The Biblical God was originally Elohim, a collection of mixed spirit forces, before becoming merged into a single masculine figure, Yahweh. El, and Baal, Ile, Helios, Allah, became the names of masculine Gods after the Sun Goddess fell from power—something She did only in some parts of the world. To other people she is still the supreme creatrix or medium for reaching the other spirit forces. The story of her descent—the Fall of the God of Light—her capture and her still-living presence is primary in Western tradition, from *The Iliad* to *Cinder Ella* to *Faust* to modern movies of tragic female stars who rise, fall, are murdered, rise again.

A few other names for the Goddess of weaving, loveliness and fire are Oshun (African-Brazilian), Chin-nu (Chinese), Kochinninako (American Indian), Arani, the fire-stick (India), Ashketanne-mat (Ainu-Japanese), Venus (Roman), Ninnlil, queen of childbirth and Lilanna, queen of sheep-folds (Babylonian).

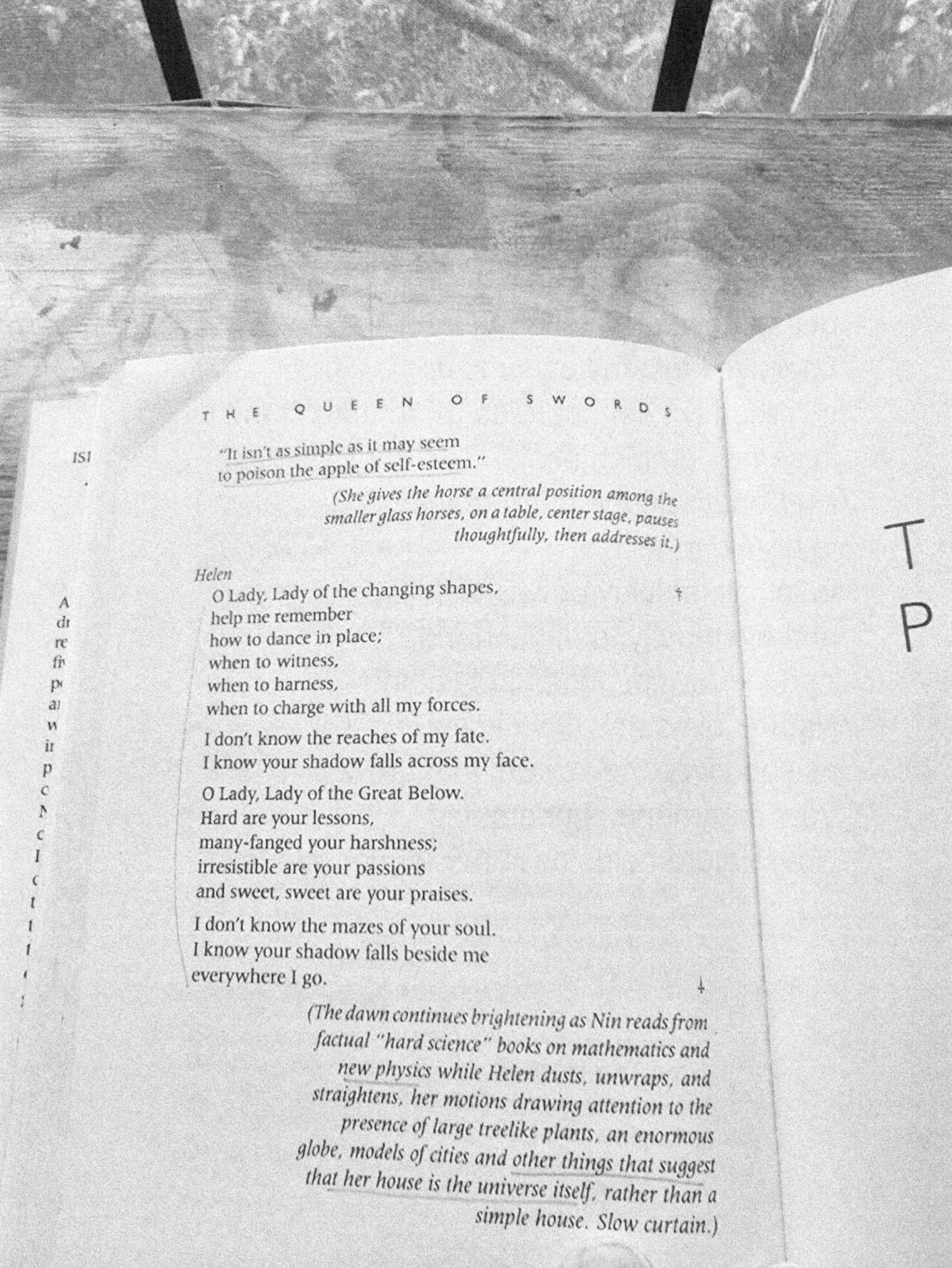
THE QUEEN OF SWORDS

"It isn't as simple as it may seem
to poison the apple of self-esteem."

(She gives the horse a central position among the smaller glass horses, on a table, center stage, pauses thoughtfully, then addresses it.)

Helen
O Lady, Lady of the changing shapes,
help me remember
how to dance in place;
when to witness,
when to harness,
when to charge with all my forces.

I don't know the reaches of my fate.
I know your shadow falls across my face.

O Lady, Lady of the Great Below.
Hard are your lessons,
many-fanged your harshness;
irresistible are your passions
and sweet, sweet are your praises.

I don't know the mazes of your soul.
I know your shadow falls beside me
everywhere I go.

(The dawn continues brightening as Nin reads from factual "hard science" books on mathematics and new physics while Helen dusts, unwraps, and straightens, her motions drawing attention to the presence of large treelike plants, an enormous globe, models of cities and other things that suggest that her house is the universe itself, rather than a simple house. Slow curtain.)

Oh, because I’m more than a beauty

Helen

Oh, because I’m more than a beauty,
I’m supposed to be in charge of beauty,
but somewhere along the long line
I believe I lost my own mind,
so recently I set out to do more than stand along
in some admiring bask,
I set out to do the harder task,
to break, to ask,
to fall all the way down,
and eventually to understand.
And I know I’m not entirely alone-
Nature loves me, this I know,
as she loves the flowers that grow.
You, a gardener, understand
How Nature holds us in her tender hands.

Do you hear the microbes singing? You must be attending or reading The Queen of Cups, Judy Grahn's epic polyvocal, ecopoetic drama of Western mythological characters interacting at a Conference. Eleven speaking characters including a cloud of microbes, a spirited dog, the ghost of John the Baptizer, and elemental goddesses like Ma and her friend Whirling (a tornado) answer urgent questions from the Queen of Cups. She is all-the-waters and has called for a reckoning in a four-day Conference of Changes evaluating values underpinning Western culture in the face of climate and other crises. The goddess of life and broad erotic powers, Helena, and Mary Magdalen with her own surprising gospel, present their compelling, heretical, much needed teachings to give us some better choices.

A selection from The Queen of Cups

Helena:

Mothers, fathers
Mothers, fathers, clasp the children, tie them to your breast
and beam like flashlights, hold the children praise them with buckets
of raspberries, shiny as jelly, give them you.
Show them they are green-worthy as grass in rain, lofty as kite-flying by the Bay,
sharp as sunrise after an ice-storm. Grasp them, study their eyes, talk to them
like kittens.
Tell them they have the sturdy grace of deer, communal peace of stones, generosity
of the sea, able, able, capable and ready. Tell them they can learn to be happy
no matter what else is true.
Mothers fathers grip the children with bearpaws of glee, press them to your hearts,
sing high into their precious ears, drip strawberry down through their lives,
tell the sons they are ships and shores, tell the daughters they are mountains
and towns that will thrive a hundred years, say the world is sending them an invitation
they just need to find the trail that's theirs.

Oh winds of change, gather the wounded
boys and girls of all rages
into your giant arms, blow brotherly breath
between their fierce sad eyes, unclench their wish
for motherly porridge, pour fatherly tears
of crooning through their bliss-hungry lips
and tell them this one truth:
when we find or make that motherplace
our vessels heal, contain no leaks
and all around us love pours in, red cells pulse
burning away bleakness
red cells flash as curious pretty fishes
spelling the words
"this is my darling life, and this is enough"
"this is my darling life, and this is enough"
"this is my darling life, and this is enough"

Another selection from The Queen of Cups

Magdalen: (to Pen)

Take your love into the difficult world,
take it without need of a shield.
Open yourself, a tender leaf unfurled,

open your clenched heart; uncurl
your metal heart, heated and then annealed.
Take your love into the difficult world.

Let go the pattern: knitted, purled,
zipped up, closed off, steeled.
Open yourself, a tender leaf unfurled,

believing in trees, sapling or gnarled,
with buds to replenish the hungry field.
Take your love into the difficult world,

the difficult, angry, wounded hurl.
Imagine planting love, the yield...
open yourself, a tender leaf unfurled.

What might to life be stirred,
what could be staunched, healed?
Take your love into the difficult world;
open yourself, a tender leaf unfurled.

www.ingramcontent.com/pod-product-compliance
Lightning Source LLC
LaVergne TN
LVHW061226100826
845148LV00004B/879

* 9 7 8 1 7 3 7 0 8 3 3 1 3 *